The Truth about Small Towns

BOOKS BY DAVID BAKER

POETRY

The Truth about Small Towns (1998)

After the Reunion (1994)

Sweet Home, Saturday Night (1991)

Haunts (1985)

Laws of the Land (1981)

CRITICISM

Meter in English: A Critical Engagement (1996)

The Truth about Small Towns

POEMS BY

DAVID BAKER

The University of Arkansas Press   Fayetteville   1998

Designed by Alice Gail Carter

Library of Congress Cataloging-in-Publication Data

Baker, David, 1954–
The truth about small towns : poems / by David Baker.
p.   cm.
ISBN 1-55728-517-9 (paper : alk. paper)
I. Title.
PS3552.A4116T7   1998
811'.54—dc21   98-2820
CIP

The Ohio Arts Council provided a
fellowship for this artist with state tax
dollars to encourage economic growth,
educational excellence and cultural
enrichment for all Ohioans.

for Katherine Girard Baker

Acknowledgments

My thanks to the editors of these magazines where the following poems first appeared:

Antaeus, "Yellow Lilies and Cypress Swamp"; *Black Warrior Review*, "Spirit Flower"; *Boston Review*, "Holiday Bunting"; *Columbia*, "Come Clean," "The Mimosa"; *Cutbank*, "Graveyard"; *Five Points*, "Ivy on the Field Locust"; *Gettysburg Review*, "Called Back"; *Michigan Quarterly Review*, "Heavenly"; *Mid-American Review*, "The Kiss"; *Mississippi Review*, "The Trouble"; *Missouri Review*, "For the Others," "Still-Hildreth Sanatorium, 1936," "Wake"; *Nation*, "Top of the Stove"; *New Republic*, "The First Person"; *Ohio Review*, "The Affair"; *Paris Review*, "Home," "The Third Person"; *Poetry*, "Charming," "Dust to Dust," "The Truth about Small Towns," "The Women"; *Quarterly West*, "The Pull," "Tract," "Treatise on Touch"; *Sewanee Review*, "Neighbors in October"; *Southern Review*, "Creek in Town," "Lightning at Night," "Violence"; *TriQuarterly*, "The Facts," "The Politics of Love Poems"; *Virginia Quarterly Review*, "Council Meeting," "The Second Person."

Thanks also to Mark Sanders, whose Main-Travelled Roads published a chapbook, *Holding Katherine*, where three of these poems subsequently appeared. "The Affair" and "The Kiss" were reprinted in *Anthology of Magazine Verse and Yearbook of American Poetry* (Monitor). "Yellow Lilies and Cypress Swamp" was reprinted in *The Sacred Place* (Utah). "Still-Hildreth Sanatorium, 1936" was reprinted in *Gettysburg Review, Introspections: American Poets on One of Their Own Poems* (University Presses of New England), and *Writing Poems* (Addison-Wesley Longman). "The Affair" won the Mary Carolyn Davies Award from the Poetry Society of America.

I am grateful to Miller Williams for his faith and friendship. "Heavenly" is dedicated to him. I am grateful as well to the Ohio Arts Council and to Denison University for their support.

Contents

Called Back   3

——— *One* ———

Top of the Stove   7
Still-Hildreth Sanatorium, 1936   8
The Women   12
Yellow Lilies and Cypress Swamp   14
The Pull   16
The Kiss   17
Lightning at Night   19
Holiday Bunting   21
The Third Person   23
Dust to Dust   25

——— *Two* ———

Heavenly   31
The Truth about Small Towns   32
   1. The Truth about Small Towns 32
   2. Graveyard   32
   3. Council Meeting   33
   4. Charming   34
Creek in Town   35
Ivy on the Field Locust   37
The Trouble   39

The First Person   41

The Facts   42

Neighbors in October   46

Tract   47

The Mimosa   49

—— *Three* ——

Spirit Flower   55

Wake   60

The Affair   62

Violence   63

Treatise on Touch   65

For the Others   69

Come Clean   71

Home   73

The Politics of Love Poems   74

The Second Person   77

The Truth about Small Towns

CALLED BACK

How it is so—

two hundred miles from a maddening passion,
midmorning blues in the sky . . .

I don't want a song to make it all better,
I don't want a home

to go home to . . .

but the tracks rattle back in my ears,
and the clouds whisper back,

and the least melody of crossroads and phone poles
keeps snagging me

with its catchy refrain . . .

as the hills recline so contentedly,
as the flocks and herds gather to their meals

someone has set out,
as the fields keep rolling on back   like cloth

into beautiful bolts of cloth . . .

One

TOP OF THE STOVE

And then she would lift her griddle
tool from the kindling bin, hooking one
end through a hole in the cast-iron disk
to pry it up with a turn of her wrist.

Our faces pinked over to watch coal
chunks churn and fizz. This was before
I had language to say so, the flatiron
hot all day by the kettle, fragrance

of coffee and coal smoke over
the kitchen in a mist. What did I know?
Now they've gone. Language remains.
I hear her voice like a lick of flame

to a bone-cold day. Careful, she says.
I hold my head close to see what she means.

STILL-HILDRETH SANATORIUM, 1936

When she wasn't on rounds, she was counting
the silver and bedpans, the pills in white cups,
heads in their beds, or she was scrubbing down

walls streaked with feces and food on a white-
wash of hours past midnight and morning, down
corridors quickened with shadows, with screaming,

the laminate of cheap disinfectant . . .
what madness to seal them together, infirm
and insane, whom the state had deemed mad.

The first time I saw them strapped in those beds,
caked with sores, some of them crying
or coughing up coal, some held in place

with cast-iron weights . . . I would waken again.
Her hands fluttered blue by my digital clock,
and I lay shaking, exhausted, soaked cold

in soiled bedclothes or draft. I choked on my pulse.
I ached from the weight of her stair-step quilt.
Each night was a door slipping open in the dark.

Imagine, a white suit for gimlets at noon.
This was my Hollywood star, come to be lost
among dirt farmers and tubercular poor.

He'd been forgotten when the talkies took hold.
He saw toads in webs drooping over his bed.
O noiseless, patient, *his voice would quake.*

He took to sawing his cuticles with butter knives
down to the bone and raw blood in the dark.
Then, he would lie back and wait for more drug.

And this was my illness, constant, insomnolent,
a burning of nerve hairs just under the eyelids,
corneal, limbic, under the skin, arterial,

osteal, scrotal, until each node of the four hundred
was a pinpoint of lymphatic fire and anguish
as she rocked beside me in the family dark.

In another year she would unspool fabrics
and match threads at Penney's, handling finery
among friends just a few blocks from the mansion-

turned-sickhouse. She would sing through the war
a nickel back   a greenback   a sawbuck   a penny
and, forty years later, die with only her daughter,

my mother, to hold her, who washed her face,
who changed her bedgowns and suffers to this day
over the dementia of the old woman weeping

mama, mama, curled like cut hair from the pain
of her own cells birthing in splinters of glass.
What madness to be driven so deep into self . . .

I would waken and find her there, waiting
with me through the bad nights when my heart
trembled clear through my skin, when my fat gut

shivered and wouldn't stop, when my liver swelled,
when piss burned through me like rope against rock.
She never knew it was me, my mother still says.

Yet what did I know in the chronic room where I died
each night and didn't die, where the evening news
and simple sitcoms set me weeping and broken?

I never got used to it. I think of them often,
down on my knees in the dark, cleaning up blood
or trying to feed them—who lost eight children to the Flu,

who murdered her sisters, who was broken in two
by a rogue tractor, who cast off his name . . .
Sometimes there was nothing the doctor could do.

What more can we know in our madness than this?
Someone slipped through my door to be there
—though I knew she was a decade gone—

whispering stories and cooling my forehead,
and all I could do in the heritable darkness was
lift like a good child my face to be kissed.

THE WOMEN

The women are gathered at the back-porch sink.
The chintz curtains say it's just evening again,
but a worrisome breeze has started to fumble
at the dish towels draped over drawers and cane chairs.
The plates are rinsed, all shelved, the bread pans
patted dry, coated with lard for the first morning loaves.
Someone has shaken every piece of good linen clean—
they should sit down to their sewing and talk.
But you can see through the fine screen the apple limbs shiver.
No catbird or usual breeze could rustle them so.

The women are bothered before any rumble
like a runner of ivy has slipped up the wall.
They stay by the windows. They watch the white
blossoms, like spoonsful of flour, twirl
among grit and ripped leaves at the foot
of the water tank next to the smokehouse wall:
like a tornado, only small, but that's where to go—
to the smokehouse to wait out what falls.
After coffee and bread the men are excused
to the front room. They nod in their papers alone.

The women look up where the black clouds
and night swirl together. Already gusts have
swept out the kitchen, drawn the strong fragrance
of permanent blueing from the afternoon air.
There's a winding of string, a straightening of things.

There's a nervous touching of fingertips to hair—
not that it will help, not that anything's wrong.
But now that the curtains are standing straight out,
there comes a rubbing of hands, and not as in cleaning.
As when something's put away, but it won't stay down.

YELLOW LILIES AND CYPRESS SWAMP

1.

So green against the standing water they're
nearly black, the sudden, wild lily stalks
cup their flames like candlesticks beyond which,
as though it bears no end, the cypress swamp
continues into steam and smoke. How
lilies grow here is anybody's guess—
an errant seed buried in some bird's wing.
Or they caught a hard spring blow, floating down.
They bloom amber in landscape hazed dull green,
darkly cool, yet dangerous enough we
must watch our step or fall upon the strange,
hard cypress knees bunched around each trunk.

And how the cypresses reach through shallow
pools for sturdiness, thickened at the base,
stretched like softened sinew. They span upwards
of seventy feet, delicate, high, arched
canopy of leaves, gauze-white in the light.
Above water their short knees go rough, dry.
Below they're veined, yellow-red, like agates
broken open or the small, torn tissues
of a body turned stone by cold neglect.
They shine in a black, clean foot of water—
mosses cling to them. Wild lilies burning
in a cypress swamp. We wish to hold them.

2.

High, lighted altar. Pews of fine-planed board.
And mourners filing past the burnished, closed
casket to kiss his photograph, to touch
the bright brass fittings, say their goodbyes now
that it's too late. When the preacher stands
to lead us all in song, we recall beauty
is most likely in these solemn places.
Not the song, too pious and commanding,
not the stained-glass lighting or white candles
thawing onto hand-rubbed ebony, not
the few friends torn apart, here to heal,
but like a sudden slash of blood in wind one
redwing blackbird flashing past a clear pane
under which spreads a fist of lilies in a vase—
like landscape cupped, held, kept. One gorgeous flame.

THE PULL

They held each other a many-hundredth time,
shaking the bed as quietly as they could.

They sailed a thin mattress warped
by the weight of their years.

Sometimes their little one
cried out in her sleep

as the stars wheeled sparkling and calm.
Her chronic, low cough swept their hearts.

That's when they saw the whole of their love
and their fear—in each other's eyes

the black sphere of a face, indifferent
at the edge, pulled deeper into the abyss.

THE KISS

Now someone's coming through the high, hard brush,
the slender river like a pulse, a kind
of punishment paid out in increments
over slick stones where the channel narrows—
perhaps it's her, slipping through the bank
of trees hung blood-dark around the cooking fire
where I remember sleeping until dawn,
whippoorwills low over fields of crickets,
a white dew coating everything. I'm waiting
for my father to come, dog-tired, angry
again and caked with mud from tying up
the boat or hooking stringers to a stump.
All the while the hub of starlight reels through
damp, black willow limbs far enough away
they look, from this angle, like tangled hair.

It's a memory out of nowhere, of
a sudden—again my fear of deep sky,
moonlight like a bruise the same blood-blue
no matter where it's bloomed this time, the one
flower rooted so far in flesh it lives.
It's a matter of turning toward one face
or the other. Now the breeze kicks up
the gold, cool embers in the low fire, and how
many stars have spent themselves spraying down
the slender dark . . . It's neither poverty

nor pain, but change inevitable as
a father's face into her immaterial,
lovely face. I'm waiting in the humming dark,
on a pallet near the flame, as one of them slips
through high, hard brush to kiss me once to sleep.

LIGHTNING AT NIGHT

The white flash blows you back against me.

> The whole sky's ablaze,
> sulfuric blues and grays,

utterly still, and for one moment we see

> things the same—
> trees whipped and shorn as if shamed,

beyond which is boiling, now green, a perilous sea

> of storm clouds
> low over all the houses.

The earlier heat hovers as steam

> above the slick,
> close roofs. You touch my neck

—it's not fear, not tenderness—to see

> if I am ready, as you are, though
> we've known

all along what's to come as crushingly

dark returns. The whole world
explodes, shattered

on its black trunk, and vanishes, leaving

echoes to
carry on, us split in two.

HOLIDAY BUNTING

He has handled the new piece like a stone,
has rubbed it, has worried the wood-work, he
has nicked with his nail the softening flesh,

and hours now in the hands of the whittler
the cube of white ash has taken on wings,
evidence of a slight, blunted beak, whorls

in the wood grain where feathers will follow,
trimmed, sanded, blued into detail, and dried.
It is greasy with the whittler's palm oils.

From the front porch it is Saturday, noon,
and white-hot with sunlight. July the 4th.
He has worked through the parade, the speeches,

the blue-smoking floats and fiddlers' show,
the town done up in flags, whipping like wheat,
the route roped off red-ragged in front of his house.

In flight the small bird is likely to blur,
quick to the air, blue wind, lost in a crowd.
But who holds it with his hands has captured

wild by a wing. Who carves the knuckled claw-
feet cut out of splinters, out of ash bark,
can stand up for himself for as long as

he wishes and bourbon to kill the close heat.
He makes a nest of shavings when he stands,
stretches, settles back down in his good chair.

And when the bird is finished, no more tail
feathers to sharpen, touch up with edging,
he will hand it around to the children

then release it to the night's keeping next
to the knife, whetted, washed, on the porch rail—
and all gone by morning, banner, noise, bird.

THE THIRD PERSON

1.

Not smoke but the shades of smoke, and not cloud-work
but the gray and smoke-green densities of clouds—
if he were sure their voices would carry through
the acre or more of underbrush and scrub,

he would call her name and stand still listening.
How can he be sure? He is tearing through the
needle locusts and grapevines, the heavy leaves
in decay over the crusted muds and mulch.

It's nearly dark, December, at four-thirty.
The woods are thick with distance, smoke-gray, growing
cold. He is trembling. We see his breath as slight
relief against the trees and smoke around him.

2.

If his daughter simply wandered off to play
with something in the woods—flutter of a bird,
twist of color in the dim limb-light and chill—
what are we to do? We know what he can't see.

She's home now. But he's scared. We must bear the guilt
of standing by his wasted efforts watching.
There is a relationship among us all
which weather, love, nor longing will clarify—

like the gray connection he can feel between
himself and the child he thinks he's lost, a kind
of vague grammar. What use if he could see us?
How can we intrude to point her pathway back?

3.

You and I know this is wrong. You are inside
rocking your newborn daughter after dinner—
week after week like this, exhausted, lonely,
you want to speak one clear word to someone far.

You look out the window, as you have for hours,
for weeks now. The woods are darker, still, growing
beautifully oblique—smoke and branch alike,
the white exhaust of winter dampness breathing.

The man is ripping through the brambles. He is
tangled, lost. He seems beside himself with grief.
Your mouth is open. But he won't hear a sound
in the smoke and gray-green distances of pain.

DUST TO DUST

1.

Footfalls on the brickwork road many fathers laid
by hand and heavy mallet make a sandy sound.
You can hear, in the dusted scuff, a kind of gasp
as from the crumpled lungs of those bent double
by depression, by wagonloads of work—
you can hear huffs of hot wind kick the dust
around them. You can feel the brickwork give.

This is how the town found a way from starving.
Three summers running: nothing but dust rained down
to choke out cornfields and wheat. The council
paid any man driven to his knees to lay
a road from here to Cedar City to keep working.
They tapped in bricks from the limekiln one season.
They turned each one one-quarter twist the next.

2.

All night, so far, I have waited for the train to come
calling through a cotton curtain on its breeze.

It always does—low as a mourning dove long minutes
over the far, darkening fields and many trees.

How huge the world must be to hear so far
beyond the shade, beyond the grasp of night.

There are apple boughs brushing my fine screen lightly.
And a dozen stars, I know, like pinpricks on an arm.

Before it stops, a train will hiss, grind, clatter
all the way back while its car-locks bang.

Then the engine at idle—hubbub, wood smoke,
and trouble in the hobo camp below the trestle.

How sad the world is to hear nothing for so long.
It always comes. Sweet night wind like cider.

3.

I was watching the road where his car went
and thirty years burned off, as in a drop of oil.
I was scanning for dust on the rise, a cartoon

cowboy's gallop. It's where he drove each morning
off to work somewhere hard with the road crew—
he returned each evening, burned and hurt.

I have a good life and hands too soft for labor.
Who would guess it takes this long to come home?
All week I have checked the old road, as if

nothing had come to pass—jars of peaches pinging
on the kitchen sill, her voice like silverware.
I was playing with a soldier and blue truck.

There's a road to everywhere, the song sweeps on.
I am watching the road where the car drove.

4.

You can feel the brickwork give beneath your step.
Each such shift in sand and balanced earth
is kindred to the world's intrinsic drift.
Cars kick up a clatter, rumbling down the road—
their tires grind brick to brick, turn dust to dust.
When a truck goes by, the whole street quakes.
You can feel your life begin to shake.

5.

Hanging primrose breeze. Haze of barbeque.
The many children quieted by baths, put to bed—

they wait for the locusts' buzz and homing trains.
One lone bat recurrent in the streetlamp glow.

Four blocks down the road gives way to asphalt blacktop.
But here the block stamp MACON BRICK hasn't rubbed off

the red clay bars the many fathers wrecked
their knees to pack tightly back into earth.

How small a world it is to want such work.
I will come here only once more to lie down too,

having lived to praise one thing made so well
it sings with each slow passage, rimmed

with sleepers safe in all their loved and many beds.
Flowers line every sidewalk down the breathing road.

Two

HEAVENLY

They are potted at night, pink, and packed
with mulch or peat, chert in handfuls at their base
for weight and hydration, they are red as day-
break is red breaking over the buildings,
they are flecked white, gray-white, and silver
like the quick sides of the sunfish that will
circle the shallow fountain all summer.
This morning I think even the afterworld
must be traced with geraniums, one block long,
for that is how far the city fathers
have gone, pot by pot, to pretty the town.
And what shall we do but admire them,

the fathers, who like their flowers have turned
fresh outheld faces to greet ours, and are
lined up in front of the drugstore, sub shop,
barbershop, the library, and fountain,
hair like little wings on the morning's breeze.
They wave to show us magnificent
flowers. Heavenly, our gift, these will bloom
clear through the summer. Let us praise them then
and stroke their soft leaves which will scent our hands
to pass on to all that we touch today—
for who are we to deny the next life,
having come far already, in this one.

THE TRUTH ABOUT SMALL TOWNS

1. THE TRUTH ABOUT SMALL TOWNS

It never stops raining. The water tower's tarnished
as cutlery left damp in the widower's hutch.

If you walk slow (but don't stop), you're not from nearby.
All you can eat for a buck at the diner is

cream gravy on sourdough, blood sausage, and coffee.
Never lie. The preacher before this one dropped bombs

in the war and walked with a limp at parade time.
Until it burned, the old depot was a disco.

A café. A card shoppe. A parts place for combines.
Randy + Rhonda shows up each spring on the bridge.

If you walk fast you did it. Nothing's more lonesome
than money. (Who says shoppe?) It never rains.

2. GRAVEYARD

Heat in the short field and dust scuffed up, glare
off the guard-tower glass where the three pickets
lean on their guns. The score is one to one.
Everybody's nervous but the inmates,
who joke around—they jostle, they hassle
the team of boys in trouble and their dads.
It's all in sport. The warden is the ump.
The flat bleachers are dotted with guards; no

one can recall the last time they got one
over the wall. The cons play hard, then lose.
And the warden springs for drinks all around—
something he calls *graveyard*, which is five kinds
of soda pop poured over ice into
each one's cup, until the cup overflows.

3. COUNCIL MEETING

The latest uproar: to allow Wendy's
to build another fast-food burger shack
on two acres of wetlands near Raccoon Creek,
or to permit the conservationist

well-to-do citizenry to keep their green
space and thus assure long, unsullied views
from their redwood decks, picture windows,
and backyards chemically rich as golf greens.

The paper's rife with spats, accusations,
pieties both ways. Wendy's promises
flowers, jobs. The citizens want this, too,
but want it five miles away where people

don't care about egrets, willows, good views.
Oh, it's going to be a long night: call
out for pizza, somebody brew some tea.
Then we'll all stand up for what we believe.

4. CHARMING

The remnant industry of a dying town's itself.
Faux charm, flaked paint, innuendo in a nasal twang.
Now the hardware store's got how-to kits to make
mushrooms out of plywood for the yard,

and the corner grocery's specialty this week
is mango chutney, good with rabbit, duck, or spread
for breakfast on a whole-wheat bagel fresh
each morning at the small patisserie across

the way from the red hotel. Which reminds me.
Legend has it that the five chipped divots
in the hotel wall—local lime and mortar—
are what remains of the town's last bad man.

His fiery death's renowned, but don't look now.
Someone with a camera's drawing down on you.

CREEK IN TOWN

Cottonwoods, willows, and scatters of wild
      indeterminate weeds high as stunted
trees, and stunted trees among the gorse grown

      hoary in the rock- and mud-banks . . . whatever
else one finds beside the creek is man-made,
      castoff, or dropped there when the river floods.

No one pays much mind going somewhere else.
      But stand still at a railing, in dust light:
shoes, bottles, a child's car seat still strapped, one

      corroded bedspring frame, skeletal, warped,
which trapped a wild dog once whose bloated corpse
      stunk for blocks, until Boy Scouts reamed it out.

Hard to believe that a mud-green creek, thin
      as a road, stagnant, standing, could swell so
high when the big river floods and feeds back.

      In one postcard, the famed water's nearing
the storefronts. Thumb-smudged, pastel, '34.
      People with parasols have come to town

to stare it down—gathered, as at a fair,
      they hold hands or point straight at the future,
the high water azure despite sixty years

of fingering, though the artist erred
in bluing what, running or standing, browns.
        The sun silvers a few clouds at their hats.

Now streets spread wide by the creek like creepers.
        Drainpipes pour down the mud bars into cess.
Tell that to the boys with their lines flung loose

        who lean over the chipped concrete culvert
and low, burnished water, nebulae of
        mosquito eggs aswirl at the surface.

Tell the white egrets, necks hooked like hoses,
        standing in a little sun on one foot
beneath the flood-scored trees they won't nest in.

        They're chalk-clean, calm, legible—like brief words
of greetings sent from the past, spelled wrong
        but so elegant we smile to see them at all.

IVY ON THE FIELD LOCUST

1.

Some nights we lay on our bedsheets
and listened for a breeze in bare starlight.
How still we could stay and not go to sleep . . .
And some nights we slipped the witness window
to gather in secrecy as in grief
on the ground at the foot of one locust,
brothers, only a few feet higher
than the dead, whom we knew to be sleepers.
Among leaves the locust was large, supple,
yet firm enough to hold shape in the hand,
heart-shaped, the scent of new dust, as a fan.

2.

A farmer's field will always have one tree
like an outpost for cattle to gather beneath,
come rainstorm, or too great to cut,
a week's worth of worry when there's
no time to waste, as this one must have been,
rippling with ivy that's all that's still living,
a few stickers, blunt limb-stubs, twenty feet
of trunk—the ivy swaddles it in high summer sun
like wet leather. Who is holding up whom?
What breeze carried us back
to a room with a handful of leaves?

3.

When I died in your arms, love, I felt small
and safe as a child under trees swinging
low limbs over the world lying down.
We lay in our one bed, month after month.
Each fever was a blessing, light kiss
of damp wind, and the sympathetic sweat . . .
You watched as from windows and fanned me
by hand. You freshened cool cloths for my face.
Who can stir without stirring the dead?
Sometimes a single finger burned through me
like a limb-stroke of lightning. Then we slept.

4.

See how the bean field broadens past the tree,
how the rows are a quiltwork persisting?
Like green bone the locust with ivy is
shoved up, out of the earth, a luster of leaves
like new skin or a fever's worth of dying,
then healing, surprising strength. I wish
I could sing a green song or carry you in branches
like light from a star behind sudden new clouds.
Let me show you a tree. It's lived two lives—
one for the brothers gathered in silence
in the dark, patting the ground around them,

one for a leaf, like a healer's hand, and the rain.

THE TROUBLE

It wasn't disquiet with her neighbors
or new house
that was nagging our friend
sleepless with doubt.

It wasn't the way she peeked at us
now and again,
checking to see how sorry
we seemed at her lone

theory of vandals or snoops—"sneakers-
into" tracking
her backyard in pitch dark, tromping
flowers, thumping

on trash cans "when everyone peaceful
and proper
ought to be sound asleep"—
nor even the way her

narrative kept angling back to
the disaster,
the day her youngest
stepped from a pond pier

and didn't float back to the surface
for hours,
and then in the frogman's grip,
who found him snared

by barbed wire sunk deep in the pond's
mud abutment.
It was all so plausible—
if pity and fright

are tangents along which to
manage a loss—
and thoroughly clear.
So why did we persist

in resolving her trouble, describing
the old
possums' habit of scooping
our backyards for food?

What kind of friends had we
turned into
to insist on the prospect
of animals, not outlaws, to

offer up deer stands,
and coon traps,
and intricate wirings of
floodlights to trip

at the slightest of movements,
when what
she needed was the pest just
not to be caught?

THE FIRST PERSON

What I wanted seemed little enough at the time.
There was snow on the ground, grayish and sticking
to the mud—the promise of plenty to come.
Snow gathered already in the corners of sills.
When she spoke what we had sensed for weeks

without saying, her voice fell clear, unwavering, soft
as the day. It hardly had to do with us anymore.
The crazy tilt of the carport across the alley
was all I could see for awhile, the weight
on its wobbly roof like a terrible joke.

But that was wrong—that was wrong. Before long
the snows shook down on what we had done.
What I wanted was to ignore it all, sit there
in stillness, shepherding logs to the fire
while the old ones went pink to white to gray.

THE FACTS

How far on one wing
    the night whistle flew

to our lives, long note
    from the railway cross-

road over highways
    and fields every night:

midnight's freight on time.
    The neighborhood shut

down to its black doors
    and blue lights. Years passed

in a mower's rev,
    in our cookout smoke.

We hammered short pla-
    cards into our front

yards each fall. Who knew
    what haunted the field

across our street, scuffed
    its small hooves through the

drying black weeds, and
    decided to fly.

It must have been great
        speed swept one deer past

a fence in the dark,
        clamor of asphalt

onto our trim yards.
        It must have seen that

scrubbed window as grass,
        a spread of meadow

or starlight, sweet sky.
        What we don't know soars

with us, without cause.
        We heard the sudden

explosion of glass
        and wild skin punctured,

and gathered in time
        to find the brown leg

pumping, a piston
        of want, muscle, bone,

feel the hot billow
        of breath drawn badly

where she lay down in
        tremors, the picture

window, furniture
        splintered, our neighbors'

house so like our own.
        Then the medic came,

a man with blue lights
        dotting his pickup.

Where we live the whole
        sky can take on the

calm swirl of a dance,
        the wind and its star

figures and those wild
        ancient myths spun with

meaning. But what can
        explain one deer, slick

with flight, where we stood
        with our facts and lives,

our late sorrows—there
        where we lived, live still.

There was one moment
        of complete silence.

We were what we would
        always be. That's when

we heard the train pull
        away in the night,

and the animal
        blood spread. Who knows why.

NEIGHBORS IN OCTOBER

All afternoon his tractor pulls a flat wagon
with bales to the barn, then back to the waiting

chopped field. It trails a feather of smoke.
Down the block we bend with the season:

shoes to polish for a big game,
storm windows to batten or patch.

And how like a field is the whole sky now
that the maples have shed their leaves, too.

It makes us believers—stationed in groups,
leaning on rakes, looking into space. We rub blisters

over billows of leaf smoke. Or stand alone,
bagging gold for the cold days to come.

TRACT

The political
trees are preparing

    leaves for the bonfire.

Scraped up with chokers
of chains, tractored to

    piles, their limbs, trunks, root-

work, earthworks will be
kindling, will come clean.

    Someone has seen.

The dogwood is dull
fog under oaks where

    webbings of small flags

and surveyors' stakes
crosshatch the spring hills.

    Soon the deer prints will

melt from the old runs
and all the slender

streams glow red with silt.

Goodbye, farmhouse, fields.
Someone is whispering

our futures into

the wind. Do you hear?
Hardhats stand roadside,

pointing their carphones.

The meaningful trees
lie down, and they burn.

THE MIMOSA

I.

Days and nights the dull metallic
                              hammer of welders' work,
unhurried as heartbeat—impact of steel, echo of flesh—
and all the summer with windows
                              braced for a breeze.

Once we lived within earshot of our fathers in labor,
as if labor were their love,
                              their longings measured
by a lifeline of shift whistles, freight trains,

the big building like a body
                              accustomed to pain.
It was our hottest summer on record, so dry
you could hear the molten heart
                              of their good earth

cool, crack, and take shape, at all hours,
the steel girders pounded,
                              fit for a bridge,
slender beams fused, bolts slammed and welded. Father

on father lined outside
                              at midnight for lunch, a walkway
of new trees planted to beautify the block . . .

2.

The air that insomnolent summer
                              rang crystal as glass.
If you were looking through glass or listening could see,
it would hold clear,
                a pink plume burnt to brittle air,

sparks that blazed and bore fruit
                              like bloom.
Days and nights
                we ate our meals, waited, slept, or didn't sleep,
and their work went on as from the next room,

the sharp silver-blue metal brought up to recast,
long hammering, in moonlight, hum
                              of a train pulling
back into night. Each flame was a radiance become strong

for some use. You could see them working,
                              silhouette on fire,
moving in a line, since by night it was cool in the heat.
Nights we carted water
                to our own trees by bucket or basin,

3.

as by day, the sun broiling,
                                        a ration of water would be gone
in a matter of minutes
                                like shadow cut down
into stone. There was nothing between us and them

but a sheet of air, a grove of new trees,
                                        and their labor
passed through it like nothing—now the groaning of hoists,
and braces breaking,
                                now the howl of a man touching fire,

who lost footing, who fell
                                like a shade from a girder ramp
in fine petals of flames and earth liquified.
Everything, even a man,
                                can be replaced in a heartbeat. You

could feel the pounding at your ears
                                        that mere block away,
all summer, yet the world seemed less predator
than forged from a flame.
                                Even the trees were aflame . . .

4.

That is how we learned to love
                              the branching and leaf-work,
the shapely persistence,
                         in the delicate fires of mimosa.
That is how I came to stand beside windows in darkness,

in such heat,
              where the hair-soft, pink-yellow-white petal
is a scant breath of breeze, even now,
                                  its wood soft as balsa
or something melted, set up to cool. I will never know

such longing as our fathers, nor
                         such labor as theirs,
nor love. But let me touch fire in an odor
like starlight, like fever. Let the breeze

black as slag
            sail the long block forever.
Faces of those I love pass in a line, in assembly,
                                      as if falling,
and all around us

the night is starting to burn and to bloom.

Three

SPIRIT FLOWER

1.

Lean down and listen.
      Lean in horror, lost breath,
   to whatever has happened in the night—

moonlight like blueing
      on the white socks, the work shirts,
   down the lines of the paperboard shacks.

   nothing but a wad of newsprint
        fumbling past a hillock

   nothing but the wheeze of a hinge
        a blown fuse

   wind in the laundry
        like a bad lung

2.

Nearly every morning, for more than a month,
      we have broken back
   through a big run of brambles

and ivy to stand at the edge
      of a ramshackle porch.
   It's the peonies we come for, most faithful

of flowers, bunched
     where the handrail would be.
   And today, at last, having cracked

fully open and bloomed
     by first light, they are so sweet
   they scent the whole yard.

    there is a moment of comfort
         in breath held too long

    there is stillness
         in the air held   air taken away

    in the sick whirling   first moment
         there is something like peace

    an absence of horror
        before   horror

3.

A trembling beneath the feet
     for just a few seconds . . . a sway
   in the sideboards, which don't even groan,

then it's gone. The leaves
     on their pitch-dark limbs
   seem to sense what it is, but they are not telling:

nor the moon pale as an eyeball,
           nor the pictures on the wall,
      nor even the shovel at rest by the door,

nor the door. What has happened?
           Lean down. The fresh honey smell
will turn your stomach.

   you are sobbing so hard
              you've no breath inside

   bending over cracked porcelain
              swirl of red waters   clotting

   you are running to the raw open pit in the dark
              panting   in pain

   too late to save anything   anyone
              dozens in the mine curled to the gas

4.

It's the peonies we have come for.
           The ants love them madly.
Cracked open

like small eggs, they are
           anything but perfect.
      Rather, like eggs, they look shit-smeared

and blood-webbed,
         or oozy, infected, flaking,
     and are sweet enough to weaken.

         imagine a town struck down by an instant's disaster
                   a cave-in deep   in the night

         one lonely miscarriage of pure grief
                   its only reply

         the earth having called
                   its own back

5.

Where have you gone, little breath?
         No one is home
     in the town by the coal mine.

Weeds poke through the slats
         of a dozen downed porches.
     Dry streets, old bottles . . .

         the ribs of a buggy
                   by a brick walk

6.

However small the gesture,
        unremarkable the notion,
    this is what we will remember:

a cluster of peonies
        has broken open,
    in one early morning of our lives,

in sunlight white
        with such fire,
    in the yard of a town where no one can live,

and we have come to take them with us.
        We have come to gather them all
    back into our lives.

before the flowering
        of invisible gases

before the dust falls
        over us   over us

and sirens begin
        to cry

WAKE

Clear stars afoam
on a black wave,
a cold night.

We step from the old
porch by ones
and twos

over yards burned
blue by ice during
the viewing.

How quickly
the family turns
to itself with grief,

and how torn away,
ice-flecks
in the cones

of each car's headlamps
pulling out
on the journey.

So soon the city,
the trees, gone by
in a blur.

We are
part and parcel
of a great recession,

souls in sequence
bearing our dead
on our backs,

like relic radiation
from creation's
first blaze—

each of us, flung
off like froth,
scorching to ice

down the long highway
out of darkness, into
the dark.

THE AFFAIR

1.

Then the long fencerow, that years ago had
heaved and buckled, took on a copper shine
in the sunset, the dew. A garlic haze
of cut pastures simmered fields away.

2.

They were flushed from sex—they were
traced with that other body, just parted.
They stood in the length of first fall waiting.
And their skin, that had been so willing,

3.

delible as ash to a trembling fingertip,
became its own again. One star, three.
Nothing good was going to happen. Night winds
lifted themselves out of wheat rows and shook

4.

off what had been done. So they turned
elsewhere. Her fingers gathered up her collar
softly in a bunch, and she put on a scarf.
It was not even cold. It was only cool.

VIOLENCE

Eerie from hung drapes, blue-velvet, dark aisles,
disturbing in its bone-deep bass echo
and speakers too big for these chambers,
the theater air quickens like blood when
a huge blast explodes from the hero's side-
arm the size of a hammer, shattering
a wall of glass over the bad guy's head.
Our neighbors have ceased chewing and keep their
breath to themselves, as the scene darkens out
into gaslights down a real, rainy lane.

Tenderness accompanies these terrors.
When the lights shift, and guns come seething,
when cars careen into crowds and bad music
slams us back with cheap force, you lay your head
against my shoulder and gaze down, or squeeze
my fist until the crushing of evil
has lifted our neighbors' hearts with a start.
Tonight twelve have died, so many been hurt
that their curdling screams have sounded like ours.
Not once have these mass killings, bloodlettings,

or this cinematic gore made us sad.
Instead, it's the hero's young partner,
his quick, lonely death an hour ago
adding the narrative need for revenge.
And not his death, really. Rather, at home,

his wife and small child asleep with their dreams,
who never knew he died and who, now that
the movie's all over, will never be
able to tell him, *We love you, goodbye,*
except in the dreams we carry home, too.

TREATISE ON TOUCH

Whom to believe? This is our central task.
My love lies pierced in the throat by needles.
She holds still as a branch on the white cot—.
It is a matter of training, of touch,

as the doctor probes the nerve ganglia
in the base of her neck. He pushes blind
with the tip of a needle to deaden
each flame to her hurt hands without numbing

her eyes, her auditor channels, her heart,
or any other system wrapped a thin
thread away against the ladder of spine.
The worried nurse keeps talking aerobics

as she cocks her syringe of medicine—
when he whispers *aspirate,* quickly she
draws it into a clear tube like good air.
Inject and she presses, she shoots it in.

To the eye the grounds are custodial,
every shrub, rose, cluster of trees clipped
or shorn in devoted form, so children
see discipline as an order of care.

The pathway through the green, medieval yards
is the same, to church or to class, and lined

like cathedral rooftops with witnesses,
gargoyles in stoneworks, stations of the cross,

the melancholy watchers of the faith,
and the Sisters of Divine Providence
laid to rest in the nunnery graveyard
only steps off the path. To visit them

daily is a march the parochial
children dread. And when she brings me to see,
two decades since, I feel the remnant fear
in the way she holds herself, and anger,

the way the woman I love is a child
again watched by the watchers from above.
It is a game to kiss the air, whisper's-
breadth over the lips, though the nuns waiting

whose sister lies still in her coffin think
the children will learn to love or fear their
own lives better, blessing the mouth of the
dead. Whom to believe? To the touch the grounds

are fertile, fruitful with pain, the needling
undergrowth, dense pollen brushed at the nose,
the figure of the martyr hung and pierced,
a hand struck in punishment from pure air . . .

Divine am I inside and out, and I
make holy whatever I touch or am
touched from . . . To touch my person to some one
else's is about as much as I can stand.

Now the nurse holds her hand steady to clear
the path the medicine takes through the tube.
They don't really know what is wrong. The weeks
have brought only pain, how the slightest touch

burns from the fingertips upward, wrists, fore-
arms, elbows, until even the muscle
mass, the tissue, atrophies. She cannot
hold a spoon or brush our child's hair to sleep.

She cannot hold her body still to sleep.
A doctor tells her, use them or they'll fail—
another thinks it best to wait and gives
her medicine though it makes her bleed,

as if miscarrying, pregnant from a
lover's touch she only dreamed she may have
known. Whom to believe? *The rays that come from*
heavenly worlds will separate between

him and what he touched.—The doctors don't agree.
There I feel that nothing can befall me

in life,—no disgrace, no calamity
(leaving me my eyes), which nature cannot

repair. Therefore,
                    I believe my love, who
lies as still as stone below her good nurse.
I believe the children walking the path,
watching the bees, and the bells which call them

to music or mass, immaculate song.
I believe this pain, which makes us all sing—,
the song like a finger pointing down, damned,
and the eyes of the faithful gazing back.

FOR THE OTHERS

It's almost nothing the way fireflies
flare every foot or so under wings
of grass on the calm lawns, like matchheads
struck down coarse cloth or stoplights blinking
blocks away green to gold on the slick street.
In answer each corresponds to the last.
Once I came to be cheek level to this earth.
I lay among others—still, glittering glass.
Dusk had gone down to dark and the usual
slight traffic stalled into one strand
of a web dampened and lit like a slip
of moonlight up the long way to the sky.

I was flung from the wreck at the speed
of light. I closed my eyes, spinning with pain,
as I open them now drawn by small wings
from the grasses veined with my form.
They rise shining a few inches on fire.
They slip back on a breeze like a breath
to float through another blank moment
before lifting, before lighting, again—
such nearness to flight, such temptation to go.
How patient they are pulling their weight
from the grass to be ankle-, hip-, branch-
high mounting the treeline to the sky.

Once I wished my way back to the ground.
I belonged to the body asleep, hurt

in the white, crumpled grasses and glass.
So the bow hurls its arrow once again
and the dipper drains its portion of stars.
I stand in the lengthening yard where we fell,
mind and heart, sunset, and the dew
but a touch of damp air at dusk. Here
the first death like a shatter of car light
speeds through the twilight and rain far away.
Here I am born in sweet grass as the others
take to their wings for the flight.

COME CLEAN

Yellow as paint
on the ribbed siding
the sun comes down.

It is how many years
and the trailers shine
in wet sunlight.

We left the little one's
laundry on the line.
You have to stand in water

to gather it in
in your flowered shift
and hair full of clothespins.

My eyes are pinned
back from no sleep.
It is our last summer

in how many years.
Whose fault it is is
no longer the point.

First the rain
then hail pounded
the tin roof and windows.

You sweep back your hair
with a wrist. The air
has come clean as cups

and the trailer court
drips with green ferns.
We were trying not

to fight about it.
Now we are trying
not to try not to try.

HOME

Again the time has come to take our morning walk.
Look beneath the heavy cedars, little dear.
Deer have strayed here overnight. Their hooves
have left some telltale moons and hearts in
innocent dry sands along our bending creek.
Creatures of many hungers say we're near.
Hear them call our human name. Like your mother,
her voice floating down the distant air
where we have come awhile, they sing us back
because they fear our straying out too far,
farther than the deep woods reach. Because we
went without her knowing we'd be gone, hear
her sweet voice cry above the others *come back in*.
In time we'll let it lead us home again.

THE POLITICS OF LOVE POEMS

This morning
after you got up,
I listened for a long, clear time.
And you know what I heard?

First, a couple of cardinals
yapping about something—
you can tell by their high, quick
repetitive chirp, like

icepicks chipping a brick.
I think they were working
on a nest, together,
in a terrible hurry

as some trucks went dragging down
for town, dieseling, groaning.
Also: more cars, a yardful
of other birds playing

havoc with each other's sanity,
the way it sounded, and a tic
in the wall somewhere, subversive,
like water escaping or a squirrel.

I don't know where you were,
but I'd guess at your desk

or visiting the night's
new growth in the garden.

     I'm not trying to be charming.
But I'd like to go on
living in the world. Many things
conspire against this—
               you have yours, too.

     When you came back to bed,
sleepy still but pleased
to find what you'd found,
I felt again the luck

     we have been able to draw on.
My body in your arms
was a slender stream of water running
along the stone creek.

     Your shoulder was
cool, the way an egg
in the palm cools
the whole hand.

     How long would you say
we lay there?
I'd guess
long enough to fall

in love again
—wouldn't you?—
long enough to drop off
to sleep, and wake up.

And when we shook ourselves
back to the populous world,
those diligent, raucous cardinals
were still chipping away

at their labors,
singing and racing around.
And, of course, the semis
kept pulling on

down into town
with their secretive, smoky cargoes,
to sell us what we need
to stay alive.

THE SECOND PERSON

1.

The beautiful athletes on the white beach
work out in unison for the camera
this morning, their muscle-clothes the colors
of berries, of bright flags and fields greening,
the sun the butter smear of wax on the
coconut palms and health spa's glass siding.
The camera loves those who never stray far,
who test the torque of their own resistance,
isometric, pure, if multiplied by
enough camp theater to entertain.
Cumulus vapors trim up in the sky
and hold still, white-veined, humid with ocean.

2.

What seems another life—the moon blooming
close in the limbs of the lake willow lit
all the low branches hanging delicate
as nets in the dew coated white in the night.
I wish I said something so beautiful
once in my life. I was that near to sleep.
I was so small in his arms he could brush
back a branch, he could bend beneath branches
to carry me all the way back to camp.
The lantern swung like a star far enough
off through the mist I knew I wouldn't be
awake when we got there, not in this life.

3.

Even the TV crew come to tape the
rippling athletes seems drawn to the water.
They stand just out of the action behind
big lighting umbrellas, adjusting their
gear, palming their brows, or they peer up
to the small banks of clouds which cover then
reveal the sun, radiant, gray, depending.
The aerobics team hasn't let up. They
step, hop, stretch their bound hamstrings, all the while
smiling to goad each other on. We watch
with the other vacationers steps away.
Some of the crew toss a small frisbee out

4.

to the waves, which catch it, which retrieve it,
white mouth. The others just stare at the sea.
The pull of the water, mysterious
blank presence of water whatever else
we are, whoever else we want to be,
draws us down as to drink, or as to death.
In the week we've been here we've done little
but savor each other's skin, in love, sleep,
or walk the costly sands where pelicans
perch on the pier posts, wings drawn out to dry.
How strong the bodies of the young, flexing
their arms, pointing toes sunward . . . then higher.

5.

How perfect your breath burned into my breath.
I wish, says the lover pressing the dark—
your body's sweet waters, silk hairs. We make
love until we are weakened, sore, sated,
carried in each other's arms as water
loves whatever it carries, as one night
under willows when the lake-wash still lapped
the bank stones slick in the dark where I slept
like a wish in my down bag. This has nothing
to do with me. His arms carried me there.
All night the slow wash of water and sleep.
We make love until our weakness is strength.

6.

The beautiful athletes sleek with their sweat
start to warm down on the fine sands—the day's
great star widens, a white hole in the sky.
The waves push all the way up to our feet
and gulls feed on what is laid there, their lives
a little economic of sunlight
and luxurious trash. We must go back
where the world is still washed in the worries
of sorrow and self. I want to keep shining
these words for him, who carried me so far—
water like a light in the vanishing
night. And for you who have carried me back.

About the Author

DAVID BAKER is the author of four previous books of poetry: *After the Reunion* (1994), *Sweet Home, Saturday Night* (1991), *Haunts* (1985), and *Laws of the Land* (1981). He is the editor of *Meter in English: A Critical Engagement* (1996). Among his awards are grants and prizes from the National Endowment for the Arts, Ohio Arts Council, Society of Midland Authors, Poetry Society of America, and the Pushcart Prize. His poems and essays appear in such magazines as the *Atlantic*, the *New Yorker*, *Poetry*, the *New Republic*, the *Nation*, and many others. Baker was raised in Missouri and currently resides in Granville, Ohio, where he teaches at Denison University and serves as poetry editor of the *Kenyon Review*.